Students of Life

*The compact guide to get
the most out of yourself
and the college experience*

*By Adrian Grant
and Marvin Thomas*

GT Books LLC
Jersey City, New Jersey
www.gtbooks.net

Published by:
GT Books LLC
66 Tuers Avenue, Suite 1C
Jersey City, NJ 07036
http://www.gtbooks.net

Copyright © 2005 Adrian Grant and Marvin Thomas. Written by Adrian Grant and Marvin Thomas. Edited by Tony Towle. All Rights Reserved.

All rights reserved. No part of this book may be reproduced or transmitted in any form or by any means, electronic or mechanical, including photocopying, recording, or by any information storage and retrieval system, without permission in writing from the publisher.

First Edition: April 2005

ISBN: 0-9765845-0-6.

Acknowledgements

We would like to thank the many people we've met who have helped us come this far. Without their guidance, we would not be able to pass along this information.

About the Authors

At the age of 21, Marvin Thomas has already amassed a lengthy list of accomplishments. Known for his motivational speaking skills, Marvin has served as a guest on numerous panels on topics ranging from leadership and student guidance to entrepreneurship. As a student at the Leonard N. Stern School of Business at New York University, he was awarded the highest honor given to undergraduates, the prestigious President's Service Award. An avid reader, Marvin's interests include history, spirituality, religion, leadership, and self-help. He is described as a counselor and mentor by those who know him.

Twenty-one-year-old Adrian Grant has also gathered a significant number of achievements. A fellow New York University student and President's Service Award winner, Adrian is known for his writing skill, which has landed him positions at numerous e-magazines. He has also mentored several business-minded high school students through the SEAD program further discussed below. Like Marvin, he is an immigrant from Jamaica and comes from a long line of teachers. Adrian enrolled at New York University to further his goal of becoming a college professor. His interests include a wide range of areas, such as computer technology, entrepreneurship and the music industry.

Together, Adrian and Marvin created the first student-run

program at the Stern School of Business entitled the Student Enrichment for Academic Development program. SEAD, as it is commonly referred to, was created to provide academic, social, and cultural enrichment to the entire undergraduate student body. These goals are accomplished by providing group tutoring, communal mentoring, interactive discussions and performance of community service. Through SEAD, students are given the opportunity to network with a diverse group of guest speakers from various business sectors. This highly praised program was the first collaboration of the authors and now, with this book, they hope to expand their efforts by enriching and bettering people's lives everywhere.

Contents

Foreword by Terrence Dean … … … … … … … … …8

Preface … … … … … … … … … … … … … … …11

Introduction … … … … … … … … … … … … …15

Chapter 1 - Behavior Patterns … … … … … … …17

Chapter 2 – "Overstanding" the System … … … …30

Chapter 3 – Utilizing Potential … … … … … … …49

Chapter 4 – The 3 Me's … … … … … … … … …58

Chapter 5 – Goals & College 101 … … … … … …65

Chapter 6 – Helping and You … … … … … … …77

Resources … … … … … … … … … … … … …87

Endnotes … … … … … … … … … … … … …92

Foreword

Life is a game – plain and simple, either you get it or you don't. It has rules and guidelines and you must know your position and how to play it to the best of your ability. Many of us want to be the boss, employee, company, victim, judge, jury, and God. Find out your purpose in life and be that!

Unfortunately we have too many people who are not educated on the game and are trying to play everyone's part. We as people of color have not been given the proper information on how to develop and nurture ourselves in this game of life. Since slavery, we have been made to feel unworthy and undervalued.

I discovered on my journey of self-evaluation that I had become a victim. I was not playing the game of life. I was playing the game of gotta get mine. I wanted to shine and be in the spotlight. I needed to have the accolades to feel validated in my position in life. I needed for people to acknowledge me because of what I was doing it. I wanted to be like others who were successful because it appeared that they had more or that they are doing better than me.

Just like I was, many of you are probably looking for answers in your life. You may have inquired once or many times, "what is my purpose and why am I here?" Each one of us has a purpose. Each one of us has something that we are supposed to be doing to enhance ourselves, families, communities, and the world. You would really like to know what secrets or answers have been eluding you and why some people seem to have it all. They appear to have success, prosperity, happiness, and power.

The truth is there are no secrets. They are not hidden for an elite group of people and are being taught in some communities and not in others. There is no educational system, class structure, or race that has the secrets. The truth is the power is within each and every one of us to have whatever we desire.

I discovered that power, success, prosperity, and happiness do exist. It lives, and resides within each of us. There is no man specifically designed with better qualities than you. We all are of the same Spirit and possess the same abilities.

In this book you will discover the rules to playing the game of life and how you can access what you desire for yourself. You will discover that if anything is to change, you must first look to yourself.

What you will read in the pages may be right on target for you or someone you know. You will read some revealing truths that may be uncomfortable for you. It's important that you continue reading the message. Reflect on what you have read and see how it may relate to your life.

In order for you to grow and mature in this game of life, it's going to take practice. It is going to take you reading the information in this book and incorporating it in your life. You will have to be diligent and relentless to take the information and use it. Here is an opportunity for you to re-learn, re-educate, and remember how powerful you really are.

Take this book, read it thoroughly. Make the choice today that you will move forward and have new possibilities in life open up for you. Declare today that you are going to WIN BIG!

Enjoy your journey and remember you are not alone.

Terrance Dean, Author "Reclaim Your Power!" and
Motivational Speaker
February 20, 2005
New York, NY

Preface

Many college administrators and faculty members will tell you that your tuition pays not only for the knowledge you gain through your coursework, but for the entire experience of living in an academic environment. As students, we tend to focus our attention primarily on our achievement in the classroom. We are encouraged, of course, to view getting good grades and a college diploma as the major stepping-stone on our path to a successful and lucrative career.

However, we feel it is important to recognize that there are, as well, other elements of the collegiate experience that can and should be developed while you are working toward your degree. What we have discovered, after several years of college, is that in addition to providing a great place to become educated in the traditional sense, this environment also serves as an excellent opportunity for developing a true sense of self, apart from academic endeavors.

Unfortunately, most students we have met view the development of their personal character and vision as something to be dealt with later — after they have received their degrees and begun to pursue their careers.

We contend that there can be no better time and place to begin this kind of exploration of one's inner self than when one is going to college. By taking steps towards defining who you are and where your place is in the world, you will be better able to make the kinds of life decisions — now and in the future — that will enable you to achieve success, both personally and professionally. By combining this ongoing search for self-awareness with a disciplined and proactive approach to formal education, you will be placing yourself on the road to becoming what we will be referring to as a "Student of Life."

In a preface, the author is supposed to tell you what the book you are about to read is about. We'd like to tell you what this book is not. This is not a book filled with the kinds of theories and concepts that would seem out of touch, or "alien" to people of our generation. This book will not tell you what major you should choose or what college you should apply to. This book will not give advice on how to increase your GPA. And, lastly, this book will not teach you how to become successful by other people's standards. This book will, however, give you the tools to make the kinds of choices that will assist you in accomplishing your goals.

We intentionally constructed this text to be a "light read" because, as college students ourselves, we understand that it is difficult for students to find the time to read anything beyond the required course texts. Although compact in size, this book will tackle some weighty topics and present you with a great deal of useful information. We believe the insights you will gain by reading Students of Life will help you to achieve your definition of success.

Though designed specifically for current and soon-to-be-enrolled minority college students, we feel the techniques and ideas we will be discussing are applicable to all who wish to conquer their fears and change their lives for the better. Our purpose is to shatter the preconceived notions we all have had as to what it means to be a "student" and replace them with the concepts that can mold us into becoming true "Students of Life"—people who are responsible for, and active in, their education and their lives, inspired to strive for their personal best, and who maintain a profound belief in helping others.

Our book is divided into six chapters that will walk you through the core ideas of the Student of Life mindset. Although each chapter will present self-contained useful information, together the chapters will form a powerful roadmap for you to follow as you work towards getting the most out of yourself and your college experience.

Chapter 1: Behavior Patterns

How the driving emotions in all of us can be steered in the appropriate direction for positive self-development.

Chapter 2: "Overstanding" the System

How, through awareness and analysis of your environment, you can develop a more open and effective view of your surroundings.

Chapter 3: Utilizing Potential

How you can awaken and harness your dormant energy in order to become the person you truly want to be.

Chapter 4: The 3 Me's

How to define and acknowledge:
1. The way you are perceived by the outside world
2. The way you perceive yourself
3. The way you really are

Chapter 5: Goals & College 101

How to maximize your college education.

Chapter 6: Helping and You

How helping others benefits you.

Introduction

What set Martin Luther King, Jr., Albert Einstein, or Mahatma Gandhi apart from everyone else? Simply put, they were able to see the world from a different perspective and make changes in their lives, and thus change the lives of others. The theories behind these actions and their strategies define both the title and message of this book.

To understand what being a Student of Life means, you must first ask yourself: what *is* a student? We usually define a student as someone who is studying and growing in an academic environment. A Student of Life, on the other hand, continues to learn and grow based on the totality of life experience, long after completing his or her academic career.

As students, we are faced with the challenge of balancing our formal education with our future goals in life. This can sometimes leave us questioning whether or not we are making the right decisions now and how the choices we make will impact our lives after graduation.

This book is designed to help place you on the appropriate path to making these choices. It will also teach you how to become a student of your own life and use all that you have learned or will learn to benefit you in achieving your goals. You may view the ideas and suggestions presented in this book as a toolbox to be utilized for your self development. The ideas in each section can be used individually or in conjunction with one another to help you create your own, personal "lesson plan," as you move toward your goal of becoming a "Student of Life."

No longer do you have to feel that positive achievement is an unattainable goal. If you are interested in making changes and are willing to take action, read on and let this knowledge guide you as it has guided us.

Chapter One
Behavior Patterns

The greatest discovery of all time is that a person can change his future by merely changing his attitude.
—Oprah Winfrey
Television personality, actress and producer

Attitude

"Life is 10% what happens to you and 90% how you react to it"
—Charles Swindoll
American writer and clergyman

The above quote points out that one's attitude is the only true controllable thing we have in life. Learning how to adjust it can drastically alter the way you perceive and live your life. As we all know, attempting to hit one of the many curve balls life throws at you can be a difficult and frustrating task. Individuals who endeavor to focus on the positive aspects of a given situation, however, are more likely to lead a less stressful and anxiety-ridden existence. It is worth noting that this kind of person will not and can not remain oblivious to personal mistakes or obstacles in life, but rather will use them as learning tools to move forward. The goal of this chapter is to show you how to take this "focus technique" and utilize it to take charge of *that* 90% of your life.

The first step in the process is to take a *proactive*, rather than *reactive*, approach to situations that arise in day-to-day life. Taking a proactive stance is simply the abandoning of typical responses we have been taught to have by society when in certain situations. For example, if you are on your way to work and your bus arrives late, chances are you are going to start the day off in a grumpy mood. After all, here is a person that is supposed to be a professional (the bus driver) who seems not to be doing his job appropriately, while endangering yours in the process. In moments like this, people often become irritated and may even hold a grudge of sorts against the driver. Additionally, while sitting on the bus, fuming, you are probably focusing your attention on the fact that, in hindsight, you should probably have taken the train, or some other form of transportation, to work. Your thoughts will most likely be colored by the negativity you feel brought on by the tardy bus driver.

Yet the driver's lateness was not something you could have foreseen, or had control over. Since you can't undo the past, you would be better off not spending your time on the bus sulking about the matter, but rather using it as an opportunity to catch up on some work or prepare an explanation for your boss. Doing this would be considered *proactive*, as you did not allow the negativity of the situation to cloud your thoughts. Conversely, focusing your energies simply on your resentment towards the driver —and what his actions have done *to* you— would have been a *reactive* response.

The next step in the process is to analyze your surroundings in order to identify those situations that would benefit most from this new approach. We suggest beginning by examining those situations where the choices you make consistently produce adverse results. Once you've located these areas, pinpoint the reactions you tend to receive in these situations; more than likely they will not produce a "proactive" (positive) response from you. For instance, let's say that you are unhappy about the "C" you consistently get on your essay assignments. Every time the teacher hands back your paper with all those red marks all over it, you feel like she's "attacking you." Your viewing of the red marks as confrontational is probably part of what is keeping you from getting more satisfactory grades. To bring it full circle, you've now identified an area needing change and noted the attitude problem. Next, you should implement the proactive technique we've been talking about. In this particular scenario, it could mean your taking the teacher's markings on your paper as corrective advice rather than as an attack, and incorporate her comments into your future assignments. We can guarantee that this improvement in your attitude will translate into an improvement in your grade. By doing this, you will be developing what is known as "behavioral tolerance"; a characteristic found in most if not all successful people. Being proactive enables you to moderate your behavior, which will become vital when you move into the fast-paced and competitive real world.

By now you have gathered that one's attitude is the most crucial element in being proactive. It is the backbone of all positive achievement and, as such, should be something we remain aware of throughout each day. Your mindset when you first wake up in the morning is probably the most important component of this, as it will set the tone for your attitude for the remainder of the day. In the same way that breakfast is regarded as the most important meal of the day, so, too, is your point of view or opinion about your "world." Here a few questions you can ask yourself to gauge what kind of mindset you're waking up with:

- What is the first thing that you think about when you wake up?
- Are you grateful for the new morning and the enormous opportunities available to you by just being alive?
- Are you anxious about the day ahead or do you feel prepared to face the world head-on?
- Do you dread rolling out of bed for fear of another day of unfulfilled promises?

Your morning mindset should be one of: "This could, and will, be a great day." If you carry that attitude with you throughout the day you *will* make it a great day. Rarely can one have an uplifting experience by waking up "on the wrong side of the bed." Indeed, to truly have a great day, you need to begin with your attitude set in a positive direction. To facilitate this, we suggest that you take some time each morning to read something you find "inspirational." In this way, the first thoughts to enter your brain for the day will be those that encourage proactive decisions which will assist you in having a more productive day.

Playing the devil's advocate for a moment, let's assume that you are one of those people who feels that there are few, if any, positive aspects in their everyday life. There's school and then, perhaps, a monotonous job. To those people we say, as long as you are on this earth, you have something to live for. Every waking day brings the opportunity for you to change your life. If you are majoring in psychology and yet feel that becoming a chef would fulfill you more, you can switch gears and enroll in a culinary school. If you are stuck in a dead-end job and realize it will be more difficult to move up in the world because you never graduated high school, you can squeeze in night classes to get your GED. The point of all this is that, as long as you're breathing, anything is possible. The only times your dreams are truly unattainable are when you cease to exist. Utilize the time you have here on earth and treasure it. In this book we will focus on finding a sense of fulfillment on the inside, because we recognize that, once the inside is whole, the effects will soon show up on the outside.

Additionally, goal accomplishment lies in close relation with attitude. Yet, in order to begin a discussion of goals, we should first define what a goal *is*. We'll explain the definition of a goal by distinguishing it from a dream. According to the dictionary, a dream is a series of thoughts, images, or emotions occurring during sleep. We further suggest that a dream is a desire or wish only possible *during sleep*. Goals are self-made initiatives that are easy to create yet hard to achieve without discipline. Only by transforming your dreams *into* goals can you hope to achieve success. For example, you might dream of owning a car, so you set goals (such as getting a full-time job, then opening a savings account) to achieve this dream. The problem arises when you notice that you want a DVD player and a Hi-Definition TV, so you dip into the savings account that was originally opened for securing you a car. Bit by bit, the goal of owning your "dream" car returns to being just that: a dream. For these and other reasons, we often find ourselves setting goals and never completing them.

On a side note, reading and following the principles set forth in this book, will enable you to accomplish your goals and find true *success*. In this particular context, we define success as the *progression* towards the realization of a dream. We define it as such because, once you have set forth a plan and are actively pursuing it to completion, you have already given yourself a high probability of attaining success. It is important to remember that success cannot be found solely in material items such as trophies or awards, but rather in the pursuit of a goal that you have given yourself. We will provide you with the tools necessary to pursue the idea of success. Soon enough, if you believe and follow through with the core principles of a *Student of Life* you will be enveloped in an atmosphere conducive to your growth as a successful person.

In reference to behavior patterns, legendary football

coach Vince Lombardi once said, *Winners never quit and quitters never win*. When it comes to making a success of one's life, no statement could hold more truth. If you aim to succeed in life, and want to take full advantage of the materials in this book, you will have to do away with any "quitter" characteristics you may have. Quitting is a bad habit and should be avoided at all times, especially if you're prone to giving up before even trying. This brings to mind another famous adage: *Nothing ventured (is) nothing gained*. If you are someone who has a history of giving up, chances are you have not progressed very far toward fulfilling your dreams.

On a similar note, "try" is a word that should be slowly eliminated from your vocabulary as it makes failure easier to deal with. It's human nature to relax when you know you can fall back on: "At least I gave it my best shot." Furthermore, it is astonishing how the faint whiff of failure can drop the participation levels in most individuals' endeavors. For instance, if your best friend asked you to pick him up after school and you replied "I'll try," that person wouldn't be sure whether you were actually going to do it and may pursue other routes of transportation. But if you had replied, "I will," your friend could feel confident that you would, in fact, complete the task requested. We suggest that you begin training yourself to replace the word "try" with proactive words like "can," or "will do." You will quickly see improvement in your ability to accomplish your goals.

In the same vein, it is important to always be working toward the completion of something specific, rather than viewing tasks as a trial or "dry run." Let's take Maria, for example — a college student working towards the goal of getting her diploma. She is prepared for the ups and downs she will inevitably face, and does not let a bad grade on a midterm, or some other obstacle, keep her from the pursuit of her degree. She keeps her "eyes on the prize," no matter what comes her way.

As long as you consistently remind yourself that you are working toward a particular goal, and view the daily hardships associated with achieving it as simply part of the process, you will continue to succeed and move closer to its attainment. Thus, you should view your attitude as an important facet in achieving success.

Imitation

Imitate: *To follow as a pattern, model, or example; to copy or strive to copy, in acts and manners.*

An interesting topic we came across in business school was the use of benchmarking. Put simply, benchmarking is getting where you want to go by following the actions of those who are already there. In our coursework, we studied how smaller firms benchmarked larger ones, in hopes of duplicating the larger firms' success. This procedure can be applied to the accomplishment of personal goals, as well.

In truth, the benchmarking concept is nothing new; it's actually been something you've done since you were a small child. Remember when you first learned to tie your shoes? Someone showed you how and you then imitated — *bench-*

marked — their actions until you were able to do it by yourself. At first, tying your shoes seemed to be the hardest thing in the world but, once you were able to do it, it soon became easy — almost second nature. There are similar scenarios in your life right now where you could utilize benchmarking. Mimic someone who is in a position you would like to be in, and, with perseverance, you will surely get there. You should consider the kind of people you select to imitate, or benchmark, carefully, as many seemingly successful individuals may lead unstable lifestyles. Donald Trump may be a wealthy and accomplished businessman, but he's also been through several divorces and sizable bankruptcies that would cripple most people.

You can even choose to benchmark people who possess the character traits you most admire. Whether he or she is a schoolteacher or a professional basketball player doesn't really matter. What does matter is that the example of this person pushes you to be greater than you are now.

In summation, benchmarking can be an excellent tool when attempting to define and complete objectives. After you have set a goal for yourself, you may want to imitate the efforts of those who have already accomplished these goals in the hopes of duplicating their results.

Function-based results

To utilize your potential, you must be able to learn from the past, and embody it in the present, in order to achieve something greater in the future.

Each and every day we go through life picking up tidbits of useful information which we then place in our ever-expanding knowledge bank. During childhood we learned that we should not play with fire and so, as we got older, we exercised caution when dealing with flammable materials. This process of performing actions based on experience is known as *functioning based on results*.

In society, we are groomed at a young age to be aware of the negative results associated with not completing tasks successfully. It's imbedded in our minds from an early age to always take the "safe" route and forego the potential rewards associated with taking risks. The educational system has trained us to believe that our goal should *always* be to attain a regular job, work hard until age 65, retire, and then enjoy the benefits of our soon-to-be-over life. When examined more closely, this philosophy of avoiding risk serves to strengthen the idea of fearing success. Failure then serves as a security blanket for people to fall back on when attempting to progress in an activity. This acceptance of failure pushes positive results further and further away.

A great example can be found in the business world, where few are bold enough to venture into entrepreneurship. Although many businesses originate from entrepreneurship, we are taught to go into the market rather than to create it ourselves. Imagine if, instead, society taught us the complete opposite —to fear failure. What if we were always expected to do the best we could, at all times, with no room for failure? Can you imagine the productivity and technological advancements that would be possible? Back on this planet, however, our society accepts mediocrity freely. It makes failure a rite of passage into adulthood, as most people give up their childish ambitions to become more "realistic." Success is thus portrayed as some kind of rare caviar only fit for some, while failure is a $3 value meal readily available for all to enjoy. This serves to strengthen the effect of the "lazy-bone," as we are trained to be content with failure, only having to "give it a try" as we discussed in the section on attitude.

Also touched on in the Attitude section was the direct impact behavior has on the outcome of daily activities. For example, if you consistently get negative results from something that you do, and you continue to behave in the same fashion, you will continue to get those same results. By employing the functioning-based-on-results concept, you will begin to recognize this behavior pattern, and make the necessary changes in your actions to provide more positive results.

Changing with Change

In this world, nothing is certain but death and taxes.
— Benjamin Franklin

We all know that life can sometimes be extraordinarily pleasure filled. We may get a lucky break, meet that special someone, do really well on an exam that we didn't prepare for, or other things of that nature that will bring a smile to our face. However, with life's "ups" come many "downs," and it is how you respond to these "downs" that will be the true indicator of your character. Understanding that things can, and always will, change will make you a more flexible and ultimately a more productive person.

Indeed, there are few, if any, certainties in life, and the sooner you grasp that reality the sooner you will be able to adapt to your evolving environment. Students of Life commit themselves to acquiring this ability, in order to place themselves into a position where they can always execute actions that will lead to the desired result. It is to your benefit to understand that you may not always be in control of every situation. However, how you react in a given situation, or your attitude, is *always* within your control. Whether you have a reactive or proactive response can make all the difference. In short, a person who can change with the environment will never fall victim to the repercussions of those changes.

Control your world.

Question #1

In regard to your behavior pattern, what are some things that seem to always trip you up while attempting to accomplish a goal?

Question #2

What will be the empowering words you say to yourself when you wake up each morning?

Chapter Two
Overstanding the system

*Civilization had too many rules for me,
so I did my best to rewrite them.*
—Bill Cosby
Comedian and actor

The System. Somewhere down the line we've all heard the term, but does it really exist? Is it true that there's a structure in place dictating benefits only to certain individuals in society? Are facts, such as the higher percentage of blacks and Latinos in the prison population, and the lack of minority *Fortune 500* CEOs a coincidence? Unfortunately, this is not a coincidence and the answer is yes, the system does in fact exist. However, there also exists a process you can go through to minimize its effects on your life. Instead of becoming a victim of its traps, you can actually take advantage of the System by subscribing to the techniques set forth in this chapter.

You may be wondering why we have chosen the word "overstanding," rather than "understanding." Put simply, to overstand implies not only the *understanding* of a particular condition, but the ability to "exploit it, break it apart, and set it back up again." The key difference between the two is that understanding is defined as having a strong grasp as to the meaning of something whereas overstanding is both the understanding, *and* full comprehension of, the entire make-up of a particular matter. For example a law student exhibits signs of understanding law, as she had to pass the LSAT's to get into law school. A judge on the other hand exhibits signs of overstanding law, as to be elected into that position requires thorough knowledge of the subject matter and all its inner workings. The ability to "overstand" the system can be achieved through a two-step course of action involving Awareness and Analysis.

Awareness

As you have probably noticed, there are a multitude of "systems" existing today in America. For starters, there's the glass ceiling, which obstructs the rise of certain ethnicities and women in the business world and elsewhere. Then there's the political system, which suppresses key societal needs (such as health care and education), through the efforts of corporate funding and special interest groups. Sadly, these two are but a few of the many systems that can be found in American society. If you are a minority between the ages of 16 to 22, there are several that you are most likely already aware of. First and foremost is the prison system behind the judicial process.

Privatizing plus Prison equals Profit

Though somewhat obscured, behind our criminal justice system lays a questionable arrangement many have dubbed the Prison Industrial Complex (PIC). Formed by a clever interweaving of government policy and private business, the PIC helps to manipulate the public's perception of the "fight against crime" — specifically *the war on drugs* — and is really a front to cover up the large profits certain companies are making from the prison industry. Furthermore, those in control of the PIC have great influence on various public-policy issues, including jail terms and sentencing policy.

Participants in the PIC come from various business sectors, including construction companies, food manufacturers, architects, transportation services, security-device manufacturers, and medical and furniture suppliers. Communications companies like AT&T and Sprint are just a few of the corporations vying for lucrative contracts that would enable them to make money off the long distance phone calls made by prisoners. Other prominent firms within the PIC are blue chip companies such as Smith Barney and American Express who, it is estimated, have a combined investment of around $30 billion dollars in the prison industry. Together, these and other groups have made the PIC one of America's prime sources of investment in the penal system, with a total value of over $50 billion.

The money tied up in this industry usually gets funneled to other businesses and organizations in hopes of further increasing its size. For example, it's been rumored that a significant component of their public policy work is ironically carried out through a not-for-profit organization that most of us haven't even heard of, the American Legislative Exchange Council (ALEC). This group consists of one-third state lawmakers and two-thirds private companies. ALEC gathers several times a year to create "model" bills, which the legislators then try to pass in their respective states.

Previous model bills developed by ALEC include: mandatory minimum sentences; the "Three Strikes" law; the stiff 25-years-to-life provision for repeat offenders, and a "truth-in-sentencing" mandate that requires inmates to serve the majority of their prison time without the possibility of parole. If you're in any way familiar with the law, some of these bills will sound familiar to you as they're probably active in your state thanks to the council. Although ALEC didn't come up with any of these laws completely on their own, you can rest assured that its members played key roles in passing these bills. Coincidentally, within the past two decades, the inmate population has quadrupled and has maintained a consistent annual growth rate of 3.5%, (45,000 inmates per year), since 1995.

Why you should be aware of the Prison Industrial Complex

If there's one concept you learn after four years of business school, it is the need of businesses to have easy access to necessary raw materials. The prison industry is no different; unfortunately, the primary material they need is human beings. Sadly, this is where you and I come into play, as our community constitutes the chief resource for the industry. According to Bureau of Justice Statistics in 2000, while constituting 13% of the general population, ethnic minorities represent 44% of all convicted federal offenders. On the state and local level, about six in ten prisoners in 2002 were minorities, with an estimated 40% black, 19%, Hispanic, 1% American Indian, 1% Asian; and 3% of more than one race/ethnicity. In 2002 there were 3,437 sentenced black male prisoners per 100,000 black males in the United States, compared to 450 white male inmates per 100,000 white males.

In an effort to maintain a steady flow of materials — in this context, people — the PIC has initiated many policies to serve, in effect, as "feeder" programs. One of particular interest is the Rockefeller Drug law in New York, which has brought a large number of minorities into the prison system. In fact, as of 2000, this law had been responsible for 60% of all drug incarcerations in the state and is infamous for its mandatory lengthy prison terms. Specifically, the law states that a person found selling two ounces, or possessing four ounces, of cocaine or heroin must serve a minimum of 15 years in jail with no chance of parole. The sale and possession of these small amounts of drugs primarily occur in lower-income urban neighborhoods, where neither dealers nor users can afford the larger quantities of narcotics bought and sold by their wealthier counterparts elsewhere.

The implementation of this law has been linked to a 27% increase in the New York prison population over the past 20 years. What is most disturbing is that, although African Americans and Latinos comprise 93% of the prison population convicted for drug felonies in New York, drug selling and use are reported to be nearly proportional for all races. In fact, the Socialist Alternative Organization cited that African Americans make up only 13% of the country's drug users, but 37% of them are arrested on drug charges, with

55% of those being convicted.

On the surface, such a statistic seems like an anomaly, but a more in-depth look reveals the influence of racial profiling — another practice put in place in order to put more members of our community in the grasp of the PIC. Racial profiling is widespread throughout the United States, and is accentuated by the notion that most drug offenses are committed by minorities. Over time, this turns into a self-fulfilling prophecy; since police look for drugs primarily in the minority community, a disproportionate amount will be discovered there. The overall effect of this is that, since more minorities are pulled over and questioned, more will be arrested, prosecuted, convicted, and imprisoned.

These and other initiatives influenced by the PIC present a sobering statistic: the African American male has a 16% likelihood of being imprisoned in his lifetime. Hispanics are not far behind, with a 9.4% probability, yet that is still three times higher than a white male's chance of incarceration. Among women, African Americans have the highest rate at 3.6%. Hispanic have a 1.5% chance, while white females have only a .5% chance of being incarcerated.

By assisting in the creation of laws targeting a particular demographic, including profiling based on physical characteristics, the PIC is able to maintain and grow their multi-million-dollar businesses by providing a continuous source of inmates. Being aware of this will hopefully make it easier for you to avoid the pitfalls this kind of system sets up for (predominately) people of color. It is crucial that you recognize this fundamental aspect of your environment.

Growing Tuition Prices

As we mentioned, there are several structures currently in place that leave certain people at a disadvantage. In addition to the challenges presented by the policies of the PIC, there is the issue of the system of higher education. High school graduates face the highest tuition prices ever, leading some who would have otherwise been college-bound to pursue other routes that do not provide the same benefits as college. In effect, this extremely high cost of tuition has formed an efficient barrier that prevents many individuals from lower-income households from pursuing a college degree.

In a 2001 report, the Advisory Committee on Student Financial Assistance found that a young person whose family income is under $25,000 a year has a less than 6% chance of earning a four-year college degree. Moreover, African American and Hispanic youth have only an 18% and 10% chance, respectively, of completing a four-year degree by the age of 29, compared to the more than 33% rate for whites.

Though somewhat unrelated, the Prison Industrial Complex also plays a role in the tuition system. In states like New York, it is not unheard of for the government to spend more money on the prison industry than on its own public universities. In fact, since the fiscal year of 1988, New York has seen its public-university operating budgets plummet by 29%, while funding for prisons has increased nearly 76%. A decade later, in 1998, the gap between these two expenditures was approximately $275 million. Furthermore, according to the Center on Juvenile and Criminal Justice, more blacks and Latinos entered prison than graduated from the State University of New York in 1998. This emphasis on investing more money in the prison system at the expense of higher education serves as further evidence of a multi-system concept, and the potential traps it creates.

Given the incredible costs associated with going to college these days, it is not surprising that many young people rely on financial aid to defray some of the expense. The catch, however, is that significant portions of the aid packages that are available consist of subsidized (meaning the federal government pays the interest charges during the deferment period) loans that are must be repaid after graduation. The popularity of these loans has led the government to disperse 69% of its funds to this particular category; up 5% from a decade ago. Moreover, America's changing demographic, sluggish economy, and rising tuition levels have all attributed to the growing number of college students that now require financial assistance. Yet the fact that these thousand dollar loans are repayable, with interest, serves as a deterrent to some people to enrolling into college.

In closing, college is becoming less and less of a realistic possibility for a substantial number of high school graduates. Discouraged by the costs and the large loans needed to attend, they choose other routes where they are destined, statistically, to earn 60% less on average than a college graduate. Consequently, a lifetime earnings gap of $1 million develops between these two groups. Judging by the statistical trends outlined above, we can only assume this gap will continue to widen in the years to come.

Despite Affirmative Action, tuition costs have become a deterrent for many people of color in modern-day society. It is important to be aware of this situation and its impact on the future when analyzing one's surroundings.

The Glass Ceiling

In the past, the government has released reports stating that the stereotypical perception of minorities was the number one barrier to their advancement to senior-level positions. As recently as 1999, the U.S. Bureau of Labor Statistics determined that the wide wage gap between the races was still due in part to discrimination and its effect of minorities being passed over for promotions. This continued discrimination has helped to create what is commonly known as the "glass ceiling" — a potent but invisible barrier to the advancement of women and minorities in corporate America.

The structure of this glass ceiling is composed of two layers, both of which are contradictory to the key American ideals of individual worth and accountability. The first layer is related to the inequalities in access to higher education — this is the "opportunity barrier." The second is the more insidious and less visible "difference barrier" — the conscious and unconscious stereotyping and bias related to gender, race and ethnicity.

After the mainstream media began to focus attention on this phenomenon, President Bush senior was pressured to form a committee to investigate the issue. With approval from Congress, the Federal Glass Ceiling Commission was born, along with the Civil Rights Act of 1991. In 1995, it released *Good for business: Making full use of the nation's human capital*, which was a study on executive positions at Fortune 1000 Industrial and Fortune 500 companies. It revealed that in both these segments, 97% of senior managers were white, with 95-97% of them being male. Interestingly, the study was conducted at a time when 57% of the workforce was minorities, female, or both. The study also pointed out that minorities were not earning equivalent pay for the same positions, with African Americans earning only 79% of what their white counterparts were receiving for the same job.

The glass ceiling is as prevalent now as it has ever been, especially for women. In *A New Look Through the Glass Ceiling: Where Are the Women*, the U.S. General Accounting Office and members of the House of Representatives reported that the earnings gap between male and female full-time managers actually *increased* between 1995 and 2000. For example, in 1995, a full-time female manager in the communications industry earned $.86 for every dollar earned by a full-time male manager. Five years later, a full-time female manager in the same industry earned *$.73* for every dollar earned by a male in an equivalent position.

Further studies have shown that African American women not only earn significantly less than white males, but white females as well. Specifically, African American women receive only 65% of the wages earned by Caucasian males whereas Caucasian women receive 72%. Hispanic women have the lowest earnings compared with white men, at a rate of 51% in 2001.

Women are certainly not the only ones affected by the glass ceiling; significant evidence has been found that black men face even greater racial discrimination in the labor market than black women. In fact, a study conducted in the late '90s found that black women had a substantially larger hire-to-applicant ratio than black men. Further studies revealed that this preferential treatment of black women stems from the perception that they are single mothers in greater need of work, and thus are viewed as more reliable. Black men, on the other hand, are regarded as unreliable and sometimes even threatening, according to surveys run by Kirschenman and Neckerman. A more recent study conducted in 2002 backs up this assertion by showing that black men are more apt to be hired for jobs that require background checks. The background-checking process helps ease the fear of the employers that their prospective workers may embody the negative drug dealing, violent, stereotypes associated with black men in our society.

In terms of wages, minority males suffer from the same disparity as minority women. In 1998, it was estimated that black men earned 71 cents on the dollar, compared to their white counterparts, with college-educated black males increasing that figure by only one penny.

The "System"

The Prison Industrial Complex, escalating college tuition, and the glass ceiling are but a few of the structures that are out there, ready and willing to leave you at a disadvantage. As your parents have probably told you — or as you have perhaps already experienced — if you are person of color living in America today, the odds are against you. Moreover, these systems exhibit no signs of changing in the foreseeable future. Studies show that over the next decade or so, if incarceration rates are sustained at the 2001 level, an Hispanic male will have a one-in-six likelihood of going to jail during the course of his life, with black males having one chance in three of being incarcerated. The outlook for women is no better— decades of sexism in wage distribution has left females of color striving to attain equal pay with minority men, even as minority men lag far behind Caucasian males.

Unfortunately, these are things that you and probably your children will have to deal with in life. As long as we live in a society that is neither color nor gender-blind, prejudice and favoritism will always be present. The world may not be fair, but that doesn't mean hope is lost. There *are* policies and initiatives being created that can lessen the effects of the system and its sub-structures.

But, before you go diving into a pool of optimism, it is important that you take the current situation as a matter of fact and not fiction. It is embedded in our culture and will be around for a long time to come. What you *do* with this awareness, however, will determine the kind of person you will become.

It is time to ask yourself: will you be the person who exists only to soak up and feed off your surroundings and thus become simply a product of your environment? Or will you be someone who takes hold of life, using the obstacles that confront us all as learning tools and stepping stones to success?

If your answer is the latter, it is time to take action.

Analysis (Taking Action)

Avoiding the PIC

Our parents always told us, "you are the friends you keep." If, for example, you hang around computer gamers and tech-savvy people, chances are you, yourself, are a computer gamer and a tech savvy person, as well. On the flip side, if you hang around with individuals who have questionable morals, more than likely it will have effects on you.

Growing up we were taught to take pride in our friends, as they were reflective of our character. We didn't take much notice of this as we always thought those who were "cooler" were the kids we wanted to be friends with and therefore liked to be around. After realizing that most of these kids had no aspirations besides wearing the newest sneakers and name-brand clothes, we realized our friends didn't share our same mentality. After all, how could we – or anyone – attain peak performance when hanging around those who top off at only 60% effort?

When troubles come your way, you will quickly find out which people were with you for the long haul. However, it is not wise to wait until crunch time to figure out who's who. You can, and should, start creating your "team" of like-minded, goal-oriented people now. We are not suggesting that you only surround yourself with people possessing similar beliefs to your own, but rather that you expose yourself to the thinking and behavior of progressive and motivated individuals.

An immediate effect of associating with these kinds of people is that it can minimize the effect the PIC will have on your life. With the nationwide use of racial profiling and the lack of racial sensitivity on the part of many police officers, you should be careful not to put yourself in situations where one of your friends can cause a confrontation between you and the law. In other words, hanging around with shady characters will probably lead to shady events, both of which, ideally, should be avoided. To sum up, one of the first things you want to do to prepare for "combat" with the system is to gather your "troops," in this case, your friends. During your lifetime you'll meet many different kinds of people. Bear in mind however that the friends you keep are an indication of the events you'll meet, so choose wisely.

Shattering the Glass ceiling

The glass ceiling is not unbreakable if you take the right steps beforehand. During a job search, you should look at the company's employees to see if there is anyone in a position to which you aspire that "looks like you." If you notice that there are few, if any, it is likely that the company does not reflect the hiring practices that you would optimally desire. This should not deter you, however, from applying to this company, as there is always the possibility that you may be "just who they are looking for."

Another approach is to research which companies are known to exhibit diverse recruitment strategies, or in other ways show signs of not having a glass ceiling. Indications of this can be anything from frequent promotion opportunities, to a high concentration of females or males of color on the executive board. A good place to begin would be to look at *Fortune*'s articles on the 50 best companies for minorities.

Prior to seeking new and better employment, it will be helpful to get in the habit of documenting career successes that are often not fully described on a resume. By reviewing your list of accomplishments before each job interview, you will have this additional information at your disposal when you meet with the human resource personnel. It may very well be that some aspect of your work or life history that is *not* on your resume will be just the thing to pique the interest of your interviewer and result in a position with the firm.

When documenting your achievements, however, make sure that what you are writing down is meaningful and not just "busy work." Although many internships revolve around copying, faxing, and getting coffee, there are ways you can go about acquiring more significant responsibilities. Tell your boss that you have a particular interest in this career field and then flat out ask for more responsibility. If it appears improbable that this could happen in your current position, it is probably wise to search for a different internship where there would be a greater opportunity to expand your duties, particularly if it is in a field you ultimately wish to pursue.

Another step you can take is to dig deep into a chosen career path and accept employment in a variety of positions that will showcase different aspects of the business. For example, if you wanted to go into the sports industry it would be helpful if you were a former athlete, interned at a sports agency, worked at a concession stand in a stadium or arena, coached a school team, etc. The knowledge you will pick up from having experience in different aspects of a business will make your resume more impressive and help you become a better-rounded individual in that area.

Whatever job or internship you find yourself in, it will be important to try and not only fulfill, but *exceed* the expectations of your employer. If your boss expects a report to be completed by 3 p.m., try to hand it in to her by noon. If you feel you can handle it, request more responsibility and specific work assignments. Working your way up from intern to "the corner office" doesn't happen overnight or without a lot of hard work. It can take years of diligent effort before an employer might offer an intern a full-time position. Still, you should always strive to provide exceptional results, as this will greatly help if you are being considered for a promotion, or to get a glowing reference when pursuing other employment. By using the aforementioned strategies you'll be able to leave a significant dent within the glass ceiling.

Lowering the Cost of Higher Education

There is no question that going to college in this country is extremely expensive. It can be astonishing to discover that the cost of tuition at many schools can exceed $30,000 a year. Luckily, there are numerous scholarships and grants available to students considering higher education. Since most students get the majority of their financial assistance from loans, we will be focusing on the various components that make up the typical aid package.

Although we will be discussing various forms of aid, need-based loans and scholarships are by far the most important to pursue, as they offer the lowest interest rates and are targeted to students who come from low- income backgrounds. By understanding the sources of financial assistance available, you should be able to leap over the high cost of tuition and land in a bed of higher education.

Currently, there are three basic types of federal student loans. The Perkins Loan is need-based and repayable upon graduation from college. In the subsidized Stafford loan, the interest does not accrue while you remain in college and will only be applicable once you start paying off your loan. The third type of federal loan is an unsubsidized Stafford Loan. This loan is *not* need-based and interest payments will be required while you are still in college. *For further information regarding federal loans, we suggest you contact your guidance counselor or student advisor.*

Besides the federal government, student loans are also available from financial institutions and private lenders. You should be aware, however, that these non-government loans carry a higher interest rate than the federal need-based loans. Even the College Board — the creators of the SAT exam — offer their own loans, through the College Board's Signature Student Loan program.

Another option is college-sponsored loans, where the institutions themselves offer loans. In these, the interest rates tend to be lower than federal student loans, but you may want to contact the college's financial aid office, or read up on the relevant materials, to check. Last but not least are private organizations that offer favorable loan programs. The internet is a good resource for gathering more information about these and other methods of funding.

This concludes our discussion of "the system." Hopefully, you can now recognize the multi-system infrastructure and its affect on your everyday life. With this information, you can actively proceed to overstanding the system and avoid some of the pitfalls it presents.

Question #1

What information in this chapter were you previously unaware of? Which statistics alarmed you the most?

Question #2

Which element of the system has the most effect on you and how do you plan on challenging it?

Chapter Three
Utilizing Your Potential

*There are no secrets to success:
Don't waste time looking for them. Success is the result
of perfection, hard work, learning from failure, loyalty to
those for whom you work, and persistence.*
—Colin Powell
US Secretary of State 2001 to 2005

"Potential" can be defined as *existing in possibility: capable of development into actuality.* We further believe that *the utilization of this potential* is what distinguishes those who make changes in the world from those who just inhabit it.

Unlike wealth, height, or good looks, potential is the one gift we have all been blessed with. Sadly, very few of us take advantage of it. For some, this may be due to laziness or fear. But it is also likely that many of us do not live up to our potential because we simply *don't know how*. It is for these people that this chapter has been written.

It is noteworthy to point out that it is important to always view yourself as a work in progress. Although one can never be "completely finished" as a human being, or fully tap 100% of their potential all of the time, there will always be a benefit to striving for that extra one or two percent. By embracing this concept, you can place yourself on the path to fully activating the potential you possess that, for now, is perhaps lying dormant. What follows are some of the steps we feel are necessary to take in order to more fully utilize your potential.

First: The greatest asset you possess is You

Simply put, you are your greatest asset. In business school we learn that in order to trade in any kind of securities it is necessary to have a strong grasp of the market (overstanding your environment) and the security itself (your *self*). This is equally applicable to prospective Students of Life. To begin, you must first —while free of distractions — recognize and assess who you are in your environment (see Chapter 4 on the 3 Me's). Nowadays, most people rarely spend time by themselves without looking at a TV screen or computer monitor, which makes this first step more difficult than it might appear. Yet how can you really know who you are if you hardly ever think about what you want or need, but simply act on impulse, responding to your basic urges without reflection?

In the financial world, the market itself may cause serious damage to an asset. In human terms, we ourselves cause the greatest harm to our asset. We've all heard the saying: "You are your own worst enemy," and it can be entirely true. Laziness, greed, and fear can cause the most gifted among us to fall into the land of the forgotten. We've also all heard the "hoop-dream" stories of people who were clearly destined for greatness, but were stopped short by their own problems and self-destructive tendencies.

Unfortunately, what is not commonly appreciated is the potential we all possess to be, or do, something truly monumental. Yes, we are often our own worst enemies, but we also have the power to propel ourselves to the accomplishment of our chosen goals. To fully utilize your potential, you must be in control of who you are, and remain ready and willing to use the strength of your character to your best advantage.

Second: Visualize the destination before you take the trip

No one graduates summa cum laude or valedictorian without years of hard work and dedication. Those who have achieved such honors knew at the outset that their goals would be achieved only if they worked to get consistently above-average grades. You could think of this principle as "seeing before being," since these individuals visualized their goals beforehand and acted appropriately to reach their completion. This same principle can be applied to most things in life. As long as you can envision it and are willing to act accordingly to see it through, the successful completion of almost any task is possible.

Envisioning your goals on a daily basis will aid you in this process. What distinguishes this from "wishful thinking" is the conscious choice you will be making to stimulate yourself into considering the *actions* you will need to take in order to accomplish your goals. For example, if you would like to become a doctor, take five minutes out of your day and envision yourself in the hospital hearing your name being paged over the PA system, or the look on a patient's face after a successful operation. By consistently "seeing" yourself at your desired "destination" you will acquire more drive to accomplish those tasks you will need to do in order to become a doctor, such as studying more in your pre-med classes or volunteering at a local hospital.

Third: Do not conform your thinking — reform your thinking

One of the most important steps you can take in utilizing your potential is to become the leader of yourself. With the ever-increasing prevalence of marketing and the media, it's easy to get caught up in being *like*, or even completely *becoming*, someone else. Look no further than the billion-dollar cosmetic-surgery industry, and its many spin-off reality shows, to see the spread in popularity of this "follower" mindset. Most of us have been guilty of going out and purchasing something, or holding a certain opinion, just because someone we admire on television wore it or said it. When we do this, we are not being the leaders of ourselves.

The pressure of this copy-whatever-is-current-in-the-mainstream world we live in makes it difficult to break out of the mold. We can almost assure you that many of your friends will begin to look at you differently as you begin to follow your own lead. However, we propose that you base your decisions on what rests well with *you* and not by what other people may want you to be. This concept will be explained further in

Chapter 4 in our discussion of the "3 me's."

We are not trying to gratuitously pick a fight with the mainstream media. It's just that too often we follow this path without questioning it, which can have a negative impact on the progression towards our ideal character. For example, we have a friend named Kevin who wants to go to college, but thinks that the only way that he can accomplish this is by playing basketball. Kevin is unaware of all the other options open to him because TV has shown him no *other* options.

If Kevin believes that this is the only way for him to get into college, then a poor showing on the basketball court, or a serious sports injury, or even the recognition that perhaps he is ultimately not skilled enough as a player, may deter him from ever seeking his goal. By allowing the mainstream media to influence you by limiting the number of options you perceive exist — or encouraging only those that are unrealistic — you could remain stagnant, complacent and, worst of all, ignorant of the true possibilities that may be open to you.

Fortunately, there are many instances of people who have broken away from the systems they felt were trying to control them. People as varied as Martin Luther King, Jr., Che Guevara, Mahatma Gandhi, and Bob Marley realized, as you will too, that you can use the system that is in place to your advantage. To do this, you must not think of yourself as apart from the system but rather as an inhabitant. Doing this will enable you to be in greater control of who you are and thus more apt to become the leader of yourself.

Society as we know it is not doing a great job of raising people. In light of that fact, we suggest that you do not let it raise *you*. Television, as hypnotic as it can be, should not be the primary source of your values. Watching television isn't wrong or right and we're not saying to give it up, but allowing it to form the basis of your opinions may not be helpful to your personal growth. The same can be said for any medium used by the mainstream to sell ideas. To take charge of your identity, and thus free your mind of conformity, you must analyze how you allow outside sources, like the media, or even your friends and acquaintances, to affect your decisions. In other words, by reforming, rather than conforming, your thinking, you can better place yourself on the path to becoming the best person you can be.

Fourth: Faith, focus, and discipline; without one, the other two are useless

Faith is an essential instrument in the process of utilizing your potential. We are not necessarily referring to traditional religious beliefs, but rather the fundamental faith one has in oneself. Often we doubt our skills or become unsure whether or not we are doing things the "right" way. We suggest, however, that it is *not* necessary to have — or, at least, be overly influenced by — these doubts and fears. As intelligent human beings, we tend to make decisions based on all the knowledge and life experience we have acquired during the course of our lives. That alone should cause us to feel more secure about the judgments we make.

To put your potential to use you must learn to focus your

attention. Whatever the task at hand may be, if you learn to focus on it as you are doing it, you'll be sure to do your best. It's not easy to avoid the distractions we can all fall victim to, like hanging out and partying. Nevertheless, those who are more able to avoid or at least minimize these distractions are more often the ones who will end up on top. Seventy percent effort put into an activity can leave you with less than 70% of the desired result. On the other hand, if you commit to focusing 100% of your energy on this same task, you will get at least 100% in return, not the least of which will be the sense of empowerment felt when we follow through on a task from start to finish. *Investing the maximum amount of effort and focus on any given undertaking will always earn you a great return on your invested time.*

Having discipline is vitally important when it comes to changing those habits or activities that you feel may be obstacles to success. Restraining oneself from indulging in those "guilty pleasures" to which everyone, from time to time, succumbs, is certainly not easy to accomplish, and we suggest you try to do this "one step at a time." For example, instead of saying, "I will no longer go to parties on weeknights when I should be studying," start by saying, "I won't go out tonight because it's a school night and I'd like to get some studying done now so that over the weekend I can have more time to enjoy myself." After proving to yourself that you are capable of resisting these urges, you will feel stronger and more inclined to resist them again, to experience that same feeling of self-discipline and control. Becoming more and more disciplined in your behavior is one of the keys to helping you achieve your potential.

Note that unless you incorporate all three of these concepts — faith, focus, and discipline — into your daily life, you will be fighting an uphill battle. Practicing only two-thirds of this formula is like only wearing only two-third's of a suit; it won't have the same positive impact as if all the elements were combined. Together, they will serve as an excellent framework for your self-development.

So, remember:
- You are your greatest asset.
- Envision yourself at the "destination" you wish to reach.
- Don't let your friends or the media overly influence your decisions.
- Develop and maintain your faith, focus and discipline.

Free your mind from the thoughts that chain you.

Question #1

Which steps in this chapter is the most beneficial to you and why?

Question #2

How will you use the techniques in this chapter to accomplish your goals?

Chapter Four

The 3 Me's

If you accept the expectations of others, especially negative ones, then you never will change the outcome.
—Michael Jordan
Athlete

To perceive: to attain awareness or understanding; to become aware of through the senses.

The "3 me's" are: 1) the way the world perceives you; 2) the way you perceive yourself; and 3) the way you really are. Understanding these three points of view is key to becoming a Student of Life.

The way the world perceives you

In order to analyze your environment, it is important to recognize how you are perceived within it. The way you are viewed in the world will effect how the world treats you. Developing an understanding of this will be vital in the accomplishment of your goals.

It is common knowledge that the initial impression we create is often based on our physical appearance. It is also used in society as an indicator of status. Examples include, but are not limited to, the way we dress, our skin color, or our weight. We have all, at some point, made assumptions about a person's status or wealth simply from the way they were dressed for example.

Understanding that a person's appearance can generate these assumptions can be used to your advantage. For example, we have a friend who one day decided to wear a suit just to see what would happen. Before the day's end he received two job offers from business professionals. Because of the suit, people assumed that he was important; whereas, in reality, he was simply performing an experiment.

Whether you aspire to be considered as someone worthy of respect or simply wish to be taken seriously, understanding that "clothes make the man" can have very positive results, allowing you to, at least visually, *dictate your status.*

Dictating your status allows you to manipulate the ideas and beliefs of the world to get what you want. If by wearing a suit and tie you can influence someone into thinking you are important, and you want to be perceived as important, then it is to your benefit to dress in a suit. Dressing differently than you might otherwise be accustomed to in no way changes who you actually *are*, of course; it simply creates a perception about you that you wish to convey.

By accepting the concept that you can dictate how you are perceived by others, you will be able to take control of the events in your life where appearance has influence. In this way, you will be able to guide the world in its judgment of who you are, rather than allowing the world to guide you.

The way you perceive yourself

Generally speaking, we tend to perceive ourselves in the same light that society does. By letting these outside perceptions determine who we are, we enter into a never-ending cycle of "mistaken identity" and run the risk of taking on those characteristics that the outside world may be wrongfully assigning to us.

A good example is America's obsession with weight. Based on popular magazine covers and most television programming, the ideal American body type for a woman is the ultra-thin, Barbie-doll-like figure. This obsession leads even the smallest and/or healthiest of females to feel they are overweight. Many decide to either undergo plastic surgery or participate in the latest fad diet. The bombardment of the images of unrealistically thin models lead some women to feel that, by comparison, they are undesirable, unattractive, or unfit. It is important to recognize that choosing to accept the outside world's definition of what is or is not "acceptable," is completely up to *you*.

With today's technological advancements in mass communication (TV, the Internet, etc.) you can easily be influenced into accepting a particular set of standards as being the "ideal." Make sure that the choices you make in terms of how you will be perceived by others is based on what *you* truly want to project, and not necessarily what your friends or the media encourage you to embrace.

In order to develop an honest and healthy perception of yourself, remember that "healthy" does not mean "perfect."

By viewing yourself as a "work in progress" you will be encouraged to assess your forward progress in a constructive and self-nurturing way. Working to distinguish yourself from how others see you is a goal that will invariably lead to greater personal success.

The way you really are

Knowing who you are is the most important gift you can give yourself. It grants you full control in maneuvering your course through life. Thus, it is essential that you acknowledge your self-identity and stay connected to it.

As mentioned earlier, we should view ourselves as works in progress, always striving for something better. However, those who have a greater grasp of who they are now are more likely to get to the end point successfully. After all, you can't get where you're going without knowing where you've been.

In defining where and who you are now, we will shift away from our earlier discussion of the "outer" you that you present to the rest of the world. Material things, along with your skin color and weight do not, in fact, define you as a person, and the activity of acquiring more possessions should never be the ultimate goal in your life. A true Student of Life is in search of the more intangible goals such as becoming a better person. Material objects should be used solely as aids in expression, as our true self is found after the stripping away of these goods. In other words, you will continue to be *you*, whether you add or subtract material things from your existence.

After deleting these material items from your definition of yourself, you will be left with the one and only true indicator: the inner voice. This voice is the most constant phenomenon in your life, even as it changes to adapt to your growth. At every age, you've had a voice in your head telling you left from right and right from wrong. You may think of this as your conscience, instinct, or simply the essence of who you are. Therefore, it is important that you pay attention to it and make sure you refer to it before making choices.

In the same way that, in school, we are advised, on multiple-choice exams, to "go with your first guess," in life it is wise to always listen to your "first voice" — the inner one — when deciding upon the many options life throws your way. It will rarely lead you in the wrong direction or leave you with an unsatisfactory result. A Student of Life stays in sync with his or her inner voice and allows it to be heard throughout daily activities. In doing so, you will assure yourself that your true voice is heard, rather than one that has been tampered with. To summarize, understanding who you are will aid in regaining control of your perception of yourself. Upon doing so you will be more able to maneuver others perception of you.

Distinguish "who you are" from "your perception of yourself"

As previously discussed, you may be led to perceive yourself from other people's perceptions; by doing so you have *internalized outside opinions*. This perception of yourself is inaccurate, as who you really are, as we have said, is your inner voice. Even as the outer "you" may change — and subsequently other peoples' perceptions of you may change too —this does not, by itself, change who you really are.

So, regardless of what anyone else says, you should always be aware of your inner voice. Students of Life looks past the perceptions of others, to let who they are shine forth with every waking day. *Trusting in yourself and listening to your inner voice* are truly your best guides through the journey of life.

Question #1

How do you believe the world perceives you? Do you accept this perception to be true?

Question #2

What are some traits about you that most people are unaware of? Why?

Chapter Five
Goals & College 101

In today's knowledge-based economy, what you earn depends on what you learn.
—Bill Clinton
President of the United States 1993 to 2001

Take it from us, when you're a freshman in college one of the last things you ask yourself is: "How do I go about making myself a success?" Often questions like this are blurred by internships, partying, and — this thing called homework. Despite all of the distractions of college, this is the ideal time for you to get your priorities in order and set up a plan for what you want to accomplish in life.

As we all know, the purpose of attending college is to gain the necessary knowledge and skill sets needed to actively compete in the world. While there are notable exceptions to the rule that "you need a college degree to get ahead in the world" (Sean "P Diddy" Combs, Bill Gates, Michael Dell), most of us will still find that, without the experience of higher education, it will be far more difficult to succeed.

But what are the specific elements that should be nurtured during the college experience that will be most useful to you in achieving your later goals? Monstertrack.com has grouped them into the following anagram:

- **C**ommunication Skills
- **O**rganizational Skills
- **L**eadership
- **L**ogic
- **E**ffort
- **G**roup Skills
- **E**ntrepreneurship

Before graduating college, or at whatever point you embark on your career path, it is vital that you have worked on the skills listed above. Furthermore, while in pursuit of whatever job or endeavor you define as "success," you should keep a running checklist of these attributes to ensure that upon entry into the world you maintain the necessary skills required.

Communication Skills

Having good communication skills is essential to being effective in the world, regardless of your aspirations. Great communicators facilitate the trading of ideas and information among people, helping to identify and clarify problems and present possible solutions. It is important to learn to be concise and efficient in expressing your ideas, whether it is in writing or in face-to-face interactions with others.

Organizational Skills

It is easy to become overwhelmed by the number of tasks you need to accomplish in a given day, such that you often end up going to sleep with only half of what you had set out to do that day completed. Clearly, having strong organizational skills is to your benefit. In order to finish the variety of daily tasks required both in life and in college, you will have to learn how to keep track of yourself, your schedule, and the time you should allot to each of your activities. Setting up your priorities will be key. Decide what is most important to accomplish on a particular day, and what can be delegated or put off until another time. Organize your life and your schedule to help you develop a step-by-step plan for accomplishing both your short-range and long-range goals.

Leadership

In life, there are leaders and followers, both thriving off one another. Businesses have always hired workers who are in essentially "follower" positions (office managers, supervisors, regular employees, etc.) yet possess strong leadership qualities. As technology brings global competitors closer and closer, corporations have a growing need for employees who can spearhead a team to reach the company's quotas and also steer it in new and lucrative directions. As such, the more leadership qualities you exhibit, the more desirable you will be to these companies as an employee. A great way to build leadership skills in college is to take advantage of the numerous activities on campus that can build these traits, such as executive positions in student clubs and organizations.

Logic

In brief, logic is the melding of raw smarts with the ability to think your way to a solution in a given scenario. Bear in mind, these are not the easiest qualities to identify during an interview, but are usually assumed to be on par with your grades on standardized tests and in related coursework. To have long-term strategic planning and complex problem-solving abilities are but two of the reasons it is important to acquire strong logic skills in the workforce. The ability to both analyze and think creatively about a subject requires this ability, as well.

Effort

When the going gets tough, will you get going? This is an important question that employers want to know, and more importantly something you should know about yourself. Are you the type to rise to the occasion or run away from it, in hopes of avoiding the hard work? In life, it's the people who are willing to go the extra mile and make sacrifices that will most often end up on top. The willingness to put in the extra effort speaks volumes about your character and, as such, should be a prime element of your life and work ethic. As President Andrew Jackson once said, "You must pay the price if you wish to secure the blessing."

Group Skills

As companies have moved away from the boss-heavy hierarchy to more group-oriented structures, the ability to work effectively with others is critical to one's success. Though clearly important, career-wise, the ability to motivate yourself and others around you is also a valuable personality trait. Becoming an active member in some of the various clubs and activities available at your school is an excellent way to build these skills.

Entrepreneurship

More and more one hears stories of entrepreneurs reaping large profits by finding new, unexplored markets or by inventing a new way to do the "old way" of business. These individuals were able to see what "wasn't" and ask, "why not?" Entrepreneurs are the risk takers in society, putting more faith in themselves than in the corporate structure. Inadvertently, they have caused corporate America to take note of them and seek out their talent for top positions. The primary characteristics of the entrepreneurial spirit are self-reliance, confidence, and an uncanny ability to manage risk. Even if you do not aspire to be an entrepreneur, these traits can greatly help you in your future business endeavors.

There are various things you can do while attending college that can help you acquire the skills we have been discussing. Among them are:

Attending Class

Though professors may not check —or even care about —your attendance, it doesn't mean that you shouldn't be in class. After spending thousands of dollars on a course, you would think you'd feel guilty about skipping your 8 a.m. class to sleep in. Though this feeling of guilt may not take hold —as we can remember from our freshman year — you need to understand that what you get out of your college experience will be dependent on what you put into it.

Communicating

Whether you voice an opinion in class or strike up a conversation with the student sitting next to you, being able to communicate and share ideas will be an important aspect of your education. Do not hesitate to ask for help; often the large size of classes makes it difficult for professors to spot students in need of more attention. If you find this to be the case, be proactive —visit your professor or the school's student services office to find out more about peer and faculty tutoring.

Remembering that college is not a war zone

Fellow students are not your enemies and shouldn't be treated as obstacles to your career. If you find your school promotes unhealthy levels of competition try to focus on doing *your* personal best and stay away from stressful levels of competing. Such pressure in college can lead to feelings of inferiority or outright poor performance. Take advantage of the study-group opportunities your classes provide, or, if none exist, start one if your own. Often, it is easier for a classmate to explain something to you than your professor. Try to make friends by talking with everyone, as this will help you form a support system (or "network") of like-minded individuals.

Being active on campus

While in school, you should try and include as many extracurricular activities as your schedule permits. Participating in clubs can help build skills supplemental to the ones you are already learning in class. If you don't find a club or group that reflects your interests, you can always — either alone or with others — organize your own, or initiate events such as movie screenings, trips, or even a charity fundraiser. Also, don't forget to take advantage of the numerous tours, open houses, and orientation events that are available on most campuses.

For more information on developing your skills through extracurricular projects, visit your school's Office of Student Activities.

Remembering that you are the customer

Your tuition dollars end up paying the salaries of college personnel and, as such, you have every right to be treated "like a customer." Demand a good education and competent faculty. If you find that your college is lacking in these areas, you may want to consider switching schools or requesting, through the appropriate channels, that improvement be made.

Keeping on the right path

While in college, students often run the risk of making mistakes that could end up jeopardizing their chances of receiving a diploma. Failing subjects or not maintaining your GPA requirement for a scholarship are examples of things that obviously should be avoided. Stick to the convictions that got you this far in the first place, and make every effort not to be sidetracked by the glitz and glam or nightlife that surrounds your campus.

Below you will find further tips on how to maximize your college experience:

- **Take a speed-reading course.** The amount of reading you will be required to do in college is a great deal more extensive that what was asked of you in high school. Taking a speed-reading course will help you gather information faster and remember more of what you read. It can also be useful to highlight important passages in your textbooks and/or add your own notations in the margins.
- **Always carry around your assigned reading.** You never know when a break period may pop up during the day, giving you an opportunity to knock off a few pages of required reading. Waiting on line, the

time between classes, or while you are commuting to campus are perfect opportunities to do a little studying.

- **Keep a pen and pad handy.** Ideas for your next essay or million-dollar scheme can hit you anywhere, so always carry the means to record them. Post-it notes are excellent for jotting down quick reminders. For those of you who are technologically inclined, you may want to purchase a digital organizer.
- **Discipline yourself.** As discussed earlier, maintaining discipline means understanding that you cannot attend every party and that some nights will have to be spent studying in a quiet environment. You should note that sometimes a distinction needs to be made between a "quiet environment" and your "dorm room." At times your dorm may be the worst place to study, as that's where people tend to socialize. When necessary, you must discipline yourself to find study areas on your campus, such as a library or study hall. Over time, you will realize that the more effort you put in to seeking a quiet space to study, the less time you will have to spend actually doing it, as the information will be processed more quickly and easily.
- **Throw away your TV and computer.** Well, not literally, but the hours you spend watching mindless entertainment, browsing the Web for nothing in particular, or chatting up a storm on AIM can be

better spent focusing on your studies or refining your goals in life. Browsing the Web, or watching TV are not bad in themselves, but you must know when to stop and get back to work. This can take a lot practice and discipline because the Internet is filled with so many different and interesting things. A useful rule of thumb you might want to adopt is to watch TV for half the amount of time that you spend studying.

- **Go to sleep**. If you are at an institution where the "fun never stops," it is easy to lose track of time and go to asleep four hours before your earliest class. This should be avoided, as it is scientifically proven that most people need around eight hours of sleep a night in order to fully function. Getting less than your required amount of rest, especially several days in a row, can leave you feeling exhausted, groggy, literally sick, and unmotivated to learn. As such, always treat yourself to a good night of rest.
- **Exercise**. You don't have to walk around looking like Arnold Schwarzenegger, but you do want to get in some exercise, as it will stimulate the blood flow to the brain and relieve tension. Another plus is that it will extend your life and enhance your physical condition.
- **Proofread all assignments**. If your school has a writing center, make use of it! Despite what you may think of your writing abilities, often a person will skip over minor errors and not notice them

until someone else points them out. You might also try reading your paper aloud, as this can be useful in spotting mistakes.
- **Don't study for finals.** Final exams aren't homework assignments or quizzes and should not be "studied" for. You should have *already* studied the material as it was presented and now be ready to take the final steps to *prepare* for the exam. You'll find that, if you begin preparing for a final exam a couple of weeks in advance, you will get far better results than those who "crammed" for a few days beforehand. When preparing, you should go over all related coursework and brush up on sections that you're not comfortable with. The more you are able to *gradually* prepare for a big test, the more likely you will be to retain the information and not succumb to stress or nerves in the days leading up to the exam, or during it.

By following the tips we have listed here, you will be able to take advantage of your college experience. Try to apply as many of these techniques right away, and steadily add others throughout the semester. By introducing them a few at a time, you should be able to see dramatic results by the beginning of the following term.

Question #1

What do you hope to get out of your college education? How do you plan to work towards this?

Question #2

What are some of your fears/concerns about college? How does this chapter aid in getting over these issues?

Chapter Six

Helping and You

We are prone to judge success by the index of our salaries or the size of our automobiles, rather than by the quality of our service relationship to humanity.
—Dr. Martin Luther King, Jr.
Civil Rights Activist

In the previous chapters we have stressed the importance of self development and other key characteristics of a Student of Life. We close now with the final and most essential component - giving back. We propose that self development holds its merit only when joined in conjunction with a strong conviction in aiding society. Correspondingly, the Student of Life mindset is firmly planted in self betterment, with its root deep within the land of community-focused initiatives.

Once you are on the ladder of success, you should look below to see if there are individuals beneath you on the lower rungs. It is imperative that you make every effort to help those individuals "move up the ladder," as well. This will help to perpetuate the cycle of success as, no doubt, your ascent up the ladder was also aided by others. When you give back in this way, the gifts *you* will receive are many, including a sense of:

- Achievement
- Empowerment from bringing about social change
- Personal growth
- Closure, from giving something back

Read on for further reasons as to why one should participate in community based services.

*You nourish your soul by fulfilling your destiny,
by developing the potential that the soul represents.
When you fulfill your soul's destiny, you will feel "right."
Conversely, when you ignore your soul's destiny, when
you get caught up in your own self-interests and forget to
care for others, you will not feel "right."
Instead, you will feel empty and unfulfilled. During
these times, you are neglecting your soul — you are
depriving it of nourishment.
When I talk to people who feel this emptiness
and lack of fulfillment, I recommend they find a
source of balance in their lives. I suggest they find
a way to "give back" to the world in order to feel a sense
of completeness.*

—Rabbi Harold Kushner in the essay "God's Fingerprints on the Soul": *Handbook for the Soul*, edited by Benjamin Shield

During our college careers, we have come across the familiar complaint that volunteerism is a "waste of time." If this is your position, we strongly urge you to reconsider. For, in addition to providing "nourishment for the soul," from a more practical perspective it should be noted that, in combination to relevant internships and a stellar GPA, volunteering is another component that will enhance the quality of your resume when you seek employment. (And, if you are still in high school, we are sure your guidance counselor has stressed the importance that will be placed on volunteering on your college applications.)

There are also certain organizations that offer students college credit based on the experiential learning they acquire while volunteering. We suggest speaking to your guidance counselor as well as searching the Internet for more information about the kinds of programs that might be available in your area.

Volunteering has also been scientifically linked to improving important life skills among undergraduates, including:

- Critical-thinking ability
- Conflict-resolution skills
- Leadership skills

In 2000, a survey conducted across North America found that more than 75% of the survey takers felt that volunteering improved their understanding of people, their ability to motivate others, and problem–solving capabilities under difficult circumstances. About two-thirds of those in the survey said that volunteering helped them to develop better communication skills, with 63% reporting increased knowledge on the issues related to their volunteering. It was also noted that volunteers aged 15 to 24 were more likely than their older counterparts to gain increased communication and interpersonal skills from their volunteer activities. As you can see, volunteering aids in accomplishing several components of the COLLEGE anagram we discussed in the previous chapter.

This kind of involvement offers the additional dividend of bringing you in contact with professionals and others from different walks of life. Though the networking opportunities inherent in volunteer work are rarely acknowledged, they are truly a convenient benefit of participation. You never know who you might meet in a volunteer situation that may be of assistance in your future career.

There are even health benefits to volunteering! In *The Healing Power of Doing Good*, Allan Luks provides scientific documentation of the health-giving results associated with volunteering, including:

- A heightened sense of well-being
- A stronger immune system
- A lessening of insomnia

If you're interested in gaining material return from volunteering, however, your chances are slim to none. Truthfully, there is rarely any kind of tangible return in "giving back." There's no plaque for helping paint a run-down school, nor is there a trophy given out for feeding soup to the homeless. Some of you may ask, "Then why do it?" The answer is simply: because you are able to do so.

As we have mentioned, a major aspect of being a Student of Life is awareness of your place in your environment. Since the dawn of time, there have been people who have been in need. As long as these people exist, a Student of Life must feel an obligation to seek ways to make their situations better, as you share the world together. As Confucius said: *We are all one race under the sun.* As such, we should help our fellow brothers and sisters, not because we expect reward or recognition, but because we are aware of our many blessings and realize that we are fortunate to be placed in a position to be of help to others in need.

Similar to tithing — a Student of Life's volunteer work is done completely from the desire to help others. The Student of Life is aware that it may be time-consuming, or perhaps even a financial hardship, to do this. Yet, in appreciation of our youth and health, we are compelled to share these blessings with others.

How to Give Back

In order to maximize your volunteering experience, you should search for organizations whose activities reflect concerns to which you feel a strong connection. If you feel affected by the issue of homelessness, volunteering at a soup kitchen or a shelter would be a perfect way to give expression to your concern. If you like animals, you might want to consider spending time at a local animal shelter or kennel. Remember, even though you are volunteering your time, you are making a serious commitment to your chosen organization, so it is best to volunteer for a group whose mission is important to you, and to which you will give your best efforts.

Before you apply — if the organization has an application process —make sure that you are helping individuals around whom you will feel safe, not only those who you would be helping, but your co-workers, as well.

Below is a list of criteria that you may find useful in determining an appropriate volunteer position:

- **What skills do you have to offer?** You will it find it less stressful to volunteer in a field in which you already have experience. For example, if you have proficiency working with computers, training elementary-school children in basic computer skills would be a lot easier than trying to teach them how to swim. When making your search, list those skills in which you feel most accomplished, and seek to volunteer for organizations that can best avail themselves of your abilities.

- **Are you willing and/or do you have the time to learn something new?** If you are trying to improve a particular proficiency or learn new skills while volunteering, seek out positions where you can do this. For example, if you would like to improve your office skills, you might want to volunteer your services doing secretarial work for a local not-for-profit organization. Note, however, that learning new things may require more of a time commitment and take focus away from activities involving your school work. It would be wise to decide beforehand if you wish to volunteer your time on an ongoing, short- or long-term basis.

- **Is it possible to combine your goals?** Volunteer opportunities do exist that will allow you to combine helping others with some of your other goals. Even a simple objective, such as losing weight, can be combined with volunteering; cleaning a park or working with babies are sure-fire ways to lose a couple of pounds and, at the same time, help the community.

- **What *don't* you want to do?** To further ensure that you have the best possible community-service experience, you should compile a list of things that you are *not* interested in doing. Not a people person? Working behind the scenes will probably be more your style and more useful for all concerned. Getting a sense of what you don't want to do will help you focus on what kind of work will provide you and others with the most mutually beneficial volunteering experience.

Once you have narrowed your criteria, the next step will be to locate places where you can volunteer your time. Fortunately, there are many people, places, and organizations that need volunteers. Here is a brief list:

- Visit your local city or town Web site. Most likely there will be a list of events/organizations needing volunteers.
- Contact your local United Way, Red Cross, or other well-known organizations that can steer you in the right direction.
- Look around your community and campus to see if there are any groups that need assistance.
- Retirement centers and homes for the elderly
- AIDS/HIV centers
- Neighborhood parks
- Youth organizations, sports teams, and after-school programs

Once you've found the right match, make the necessary phone calls and set up a meeting; don't forget to bring your heart and an enthusiastic spirit to your volunteer service. We can assure you that the experience will be invaluable!

When to Give Back

No better time than the present! Trying to find the "right time" is simply a way to put something on the back burner and never do it. As full-time college students we've found volunteering at least once a month to be very effective, considering our busy schedules. We have found that weekends, in particular, are usually less cluttered and consequently a good time for volunteering. The few hours of volunteering you put in each month, multiplied by twelve for the year, can have a profound effect and will be greatly appreciated. It is definitely worth your time.

If you are unsure where to volunteer, you may want to use a search engine on the Internet to look for charitable organizations. Some key terms to use in your search would be: *volunteer, nonprofit,* and *charity.*

Act Now

You may by now already have ideas swirling around in your head as to how you can get started on becoming a Student of Life. It is our hope that we have helped energize you to begin employing the techniques and ideas we have presented as soon as you can, and that you will not let the Student of Life concept pass you by.

We wrote this book in the absolute belief that the benefits of becoming a Student of Life are great, and that they will continue to enrich you in every aspect of your life. They have energized and inspired us and we know that, with time and dedication, they will do the same for you, as well.

Question #1

What are the things you are grateful for and how can you use the spirit of giving back to help others receive this?

Question #2

How do you think that volunteering can help you?

Resources

United Negro College Fund
8260 Willow Oaks Corporate Drive
P.O. Box 10444
Fairfax, VA 22031-8044
(800) 331-2244
www.uncf.org

Hispanic College Fund, Inc.
1717 Pennsylvania Avenue NW
Suite 460
Washington, DC 20006
(800) 644-4223
www.hispanicfund.org

The College Board Headquarters
45 Columbus Avenue
New York, NY 10023
(212) 713-8000
www.collegeboard.com

The CollegeBound Network
1200 South Avenue, #202
Staten Island, NY 10314
(718) 761-4800
www.collegebound.net

FinAid Page, LLC
PO Box 81620
Pittsburgh, PA 15217
Fax number: (412) 422-6189
www.finaid.org

National Merit Scholarship Corporation
1560 Sherman Avenue Suite 200
Evanston, Illinois 60201-4897
(847) 866-5100
www.nationalmerit.org

INROADS, Inc.
10 South Broadway, Suite 700
St. Louis, Missouri 63102
(314) 241-7488
www.inroads.org

Sponsors for Educational Opportunity
Executive Office
23 Gramercy Park South
New York, NY 10003
(212) 979-2040
www.seo-ny.org

The S.E.A.D. Program
Attn: Young Leaders Program
40 West 4th Street, Suite 800
New York, NY 10012-1118
www.stern.nyu.edu/~sead

Peterson's
Princeton Pike Corporate Center
2000 Lenox Drive
P.O. Box 67005
Lawrenceville, NJ 08648
(609) 896-1800

The National Foundation for Teaching Entrepreneurship
120 Wall Street, 29th Floor
New York, NY 10005
(212) 232-3333
www.nfte.com

Black Issues In Higher Education
10520 Warwick Avenue, Suite B-8
Fairfax, VA 22030-3136
(800) 783-3199
(703) 385-2981
www.blackissues.com

ASPIRA National Office (for Latino Development)
1444 I Street, NW Suite 800
Washington, DC 20005
(202) 835-3600
www.aspira.org

Congressional Hispanic Caucus Institute
911 2nd Street NE
Washington, DC 20002
(800) EXCEL-DC
(202) 543-1771
www.chci.org/chciyouth

Grant Seeker Pro Inc
1057 E. Imperial Hwy
Suite # 420
Placentia, CA 92870
(714) 577-5386
www.college-scholarships-grants.biz

National Black Law Students Association
1225 11th Street N.W.
Washington, D.C. 20001-4217
www.nblsa.org

National Association for the
    Advancement of Colored People
4805 Mt. Hope Drive
Baltimore Maryland 21215
Toll Free: (877) NAACP-98
www.naacp.org

The National Urban League, Inc.
120 Wall Street
New York, NY 10005
(212) 558-5300
www.nul.org

National Association of Black Accountants Inc.
7249 A Hanover Parkway
Greenbelt, Maryland 20770
(301) 474-NABA
www.nabainc.org

Hispanic Scholarship Fund, Headquarters
55 Second Street, Suite 1500
San Francisco, CA 94105
(877) 473-4636
www.hsf.net

National Hispanic Business Association
1712 E. Riverside Dr. #208
Austin, TX 78741
(512) 495-9511
www.nhba.org

College View Hobsons Office
10200 Alliance Road, Suite 301
Cincinnati, OH 45242
(800) 927-8439
www.collegeview.com

Black Students.com
Diversity City Media
225 West 3rd Street, Suite #203
Long Beach, CA 90802
(562) 209-0616
www.blackstudents.com

Endnotes

Lawrence, Barbara K. *Dollars & Sense, The Cost Effectiveness of Small Schools*. Cincinnati, OH: KnowledgeWorks Foundation, 2002.

Andrew, Sum and Garth Mangum, et al. *The Young, the Restless and the Jobless: The Case for a National Jobs Stimulus Program Targeted on America's Young Adults*. Policy Issues Monograph 02-01, Sar Levitan Center for Social Policy Studies, John Hopkins University, 2002.

Greene, Jay P. *High School Graduation Rates in the United States*. New York, NY: Center for Civic Innovation at the Manhattan Institute, 2001.

Balfanz, Robert and Nellie Legters. *How Many Central City High Schools Have a Severe Dropout Problem, Where are They Located, and Who Attends Them?* Initial Estimates Using the Common Core of Data. Cambridge, MA: Harvard University Graduate School of Education and Achieve Incorporated, 2001.

Poe-Yamagata, Eileen and Michael Jones. *And Justice for Some*. Washington, DC: National Council on Crime and Delinquency and Building Blocks for Youth, 2000.

Advisory Committee on Student Financial Assistance. *Access Denied: Restoring the Nation's Commitment to Equal Educational Opportunity*. Washington, DC: Advisory Committee on Student Financial Assistance, 2001.

U.S. Department of Education. *Digest of Education Statistics*. Washington, DC: National Center for Education Statistics, 2001.

Mandatory Sentencing Laws and Drug Offenders in New York State. New York: The Correctional Association of New York, 1998.

Anderson, Deborah and David Shapiro. *Racial Differences in Access to High-Paying Jobs and the Wage Gap Between Black and White Women*. Industrial and Labor Relations Review 49 (2), pp. 273-286, 1996.

Kilbourne, Barbara and Paula England et al. *Effects of Individual, Occupational, and Industrial Characteristics on Earnings: Intersections of Race and Gender*. Social Forces 72 (4), pp. 1149-1176, June 1994.

Holzer, Harry J., Steven Raphael, et al. *Perceived Criminality, Criminal Background Checks and the Racial Hiring Practices of Employers.* Joint Center for Poverty Research, 2002.

Bonczar, Thomas P., and Allen J. Beck. *Lifetime Likelihood of Going to State or Federal Prison.* Bureau of Justice Statistics. 9 Aug. 2004 < www.ojp.usdoj.gov/bjs/pub/ascii/llgsfp.txt>

Rennison, Callie Marie. *Criminal Victimization 2002.* U.S. Department of Justice. 9 Aug. 2004 <http://www.ojp.usdoj.gov/bjs/pub/ascii/cv00.txt>.

Rennison, Callie Marie. *Criminal Victimization 2001: Changes 1997-98 with Trends 1993-98.* U.S. Department of Justice. 9 Aug. 2004 <http://www.ojp.usdoj.gov/bjs/pub/ascii/cv98.txt>.

USDJ, Bureau of Justice Statistics. *Corrections Statistics: U.S. Prison Population Rises 2.6 Percent During 2002.* 9 Aug. 2004 <http://www.ojp.usdoj.gov/bjs/pub/press/p02pr.htm>

Kirschenman, Joleen and Kathryn Neckerman. *We'd Love to Hire Them But...The Meaning of Race for Employers.* The Urban Underclass, edited by C. Jencks and P.E. Peterson, pp. 203-232. Washington, DC: Brookings Institution, 1991.

United States Census Bureau. *The Black Population in the United States: March 1998 (Update) PPL-103.* 1999. Bureau of Labor Statistics, Usual Weekly Earnings of Wage and Salary Workers, First Quarter 1999.

Bonczar, Thomas. *Prevalence of Imprisonment in the U.S. Population, 1974-2001.* Washington, DC: Office of Justice Programs - Bureau of Justice Statistics, 2003.

Wagner, Peter. *The Prison Index: Taking the Pulse of the Crime Control Industry.* Northampton: Western Prison Project and the Prison Policy Initiative. 2003.

Goldberg, Eve and Evans, Linda. *The Prison Industrial Complex and the Global Economy.* Prison Activist Resource Center. 8 Aug. 2004 <http://www.prisonactivist.org/crisis/evans-goldberg.html>.

Prisons Shut Down the Prison-Industrial Complex. International Action Center. 8 Aug. 2004 <http://www.thirdworldtraveler.com/Prison_System/ShutDown_PrisonIndustry.html>.

American RadioWorks : Corrections Inc - Corporate-Sponsored Crime Laws, page 1. American RadioWorks. 16 Aug. 2004 <http://americanradioworks.publicradio.org/features/corrections/laws3.html>.

Harrison, Paige M. *Bureau of Justice Statistics Prisoners in 2002.* U.S. Department of Justice - Office of Justice. 16 Aug. 2004 <http://www.ojp.usdoj.gov/bjs/abstract/p02.htm>

Cantave, Cassandra and Harrison, Roderick. *Joint Center:: DataBank.* Updated August 2003. Joint Center for Political and Economic Studies. 16 Aug. 2004 <http://www.jointcenter.org/DB/factsheet/correctionalsys.htm>.

James, Doris J. *Bureau of Justice Statistics Profile of Jail Inmates, 2002.* U.S. Department of Justice - Office of Justice. 16 Aug. 2004 <http://www.ojp.usdoj.gov/bjs/abstract/pji02.htm>.

Drug Policy Alliance: Rockefeller Drug Laws. Drug Policy Alliance. 18 Aug. 2004 <http://www.drugpolicy.org/statebystate/newyork/rockefellerd>.

Hernandez, Eva. *Racial Profiling: A Tool of the System.* The Socialist Alternative. 18 Aug. 2004 <http://www.socialistalternative.org/justice23/7.html>.

Cost of College - rising college tuition costs, admission price. The College Board. Updated 19 Oct. 2004. 20 Aug. 2004 <http://www.collegeboard.com/article/0,3868,6-29-0-4494,00.html cb_trends_aid_2003>.

Day, Jennifer and Newburger, Eric. *The Big Payoff: Educational Attainment and Synthetic Estimates of Work-Life Earnings.* The U.S. Census Bureau. 29 Aug. 2004 <http://www.census.gov/prod/2002pubs/p23-210.pdf>.

A SOLID INVESTMENT: Recommendations of the Federal Glass Ceiling Commission. Federal Glass Ceiling Commission. 27 Aug. 2004. <http://www.ilr.cornell.edu/library/downloads/keyWorkplaceDocuments/GlassCeilingRecommendations.pdf >.

A New Look Through the Glass Ceiling: Where are the Women? Posted January 2002. U.S. General Accounting Office. 26 Aug. 2004. <http://www.house.gov/maloney/issues/womenscaucus/glassceiling.pdf>.

Differences in women's and men's earnings by race and Hispanic origin,

MLR: The Editor's Desk. U.S. Department of Labor. 29 Aug. 2004
<http://www.bls.gov/opub/ted/2003/oct/wk3/art03.htm
http://www.givingandvolunteering.ca/pdf/factsheets/Benefits_of_Volunteering.pdf

Printed in the United States
29494LVS00002B/157-1008